For

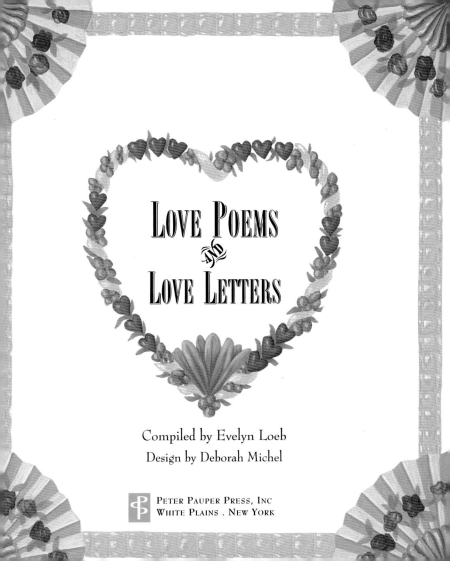

LOVE POEMS
AND
LOVE LETTERS

Compiled by Evelyn Loeb

Design by Deborah Michel

PETER PAUPER PRESS, INC
WHITE PLAINS . NEW YORK

Copyright © 1994
Peter Pauper Press, Inc.
202 Mamaroneck Avenue
White Plains, NY 10601
All rights reserved
ISBN 0-88088-875-X
Printed in Singapore
7 6 5 4 3 2 1

Jacket background painting by Linda DeVito Soltis
Jacket inset painting by Grace De Vito

CONTENTS

Dear Reader ♥ 5

Sonnet ♥ 6

Sonnet ♥ 7

Love Letter from Napoleon to Josephine ♥ 8

The Owl and the Pussy-Cat ♥ 10

Sonnet ♥ 12

Keats to Fanny Brawne ♥ 13

When a Belovèd Hand ♥ 14

A Red, Red Rose ♥ 16

The Passionate Shepherd to His Love ♥ 18

June ♥ 20

A Stolen Kiss ♥ 21

Queen Victoria in a Letter to Her Uncle Leopold ♥ 22

One-And-Twenty ♥ 24

Let Me Not to the Marriage of True Minds ♥ 26

Nelson to Lady Hamilton ♥ 27

Annabel Lee ♥ 28

I think true love is never blind… ♥ 31

Byron to the Countess Guiccioli ♥ 32

We'll Go No More ♥ 34

Napoleon to Josephine ♥ 36

Give All to Love ♥ 38

Love ♥ 41

Ludwig van Beethoven to the "Immortal Beloved" ♥ 44

My sun and stars are you ♥ 48

To My Dear and Loving Husband ♥ 49

Gather Ye Rosebuds ♥ 50

Czar Nicholas II to the Czarina Alexandra ♥ 52

Believe Me If All Those Endearing Young Charms ♥ 54

DEAR READER:

This little volume has been published in a desire to celebrate Love throughout the year, for true sentiment need know no single Valentine's Day, but rather should flourish and deepen each day. May Cupid speed it on its journey, and St. Valentine, patron saint of lovers, bless the true in heart!

Sonnet

Shall I compare thee to a Summer's day?
Thou art more lovely and more temperate:
Rough winds do shake the darling buds of May,
And Summer's lease hath all too short a date:
Sometime too hot the eye of heaven shines,
And often is his gold complexion dimmed;
And every fair from fair sometime declines,
By chance or nature's changing course untrimmed:
But thy eternal Summer shall not fade
Nor lose possession of that fair thou owest;
Nor shall Death brag thou wanderest in his shade,
When in eternal lines to time thou growest:
So long as men can breathe, or eyes can see,
So long lives this, and this gives life to thee.

WILLIAM SHAKESPEARE

SONNET

If thou must love me, let it be for naught
Except for love's sake only. Do not say
"I love her for her smile—her look—her way
Of speaking gently,—for a trick of thought
That falls in well with mine, and certes brought
A sense of pleasant ease on such a day"—
For these things in themselves, Belovèd, may
Be changed, or change for thee,—and love, so
    wrought,
May be unwrought so. Neither love me for
Thine own dear pity's wiping my cheeks dry,
Since one might well forget to weep who bore
Thy comfort long, and lose thy love thereby.
But love me for love's sake, that evermore
Thou may'st love on, through love's eternity.

ELIZABETH BARRETT BROWNING

Love Letter
from Napoleon
to Josephine

I don't love you, not at all; on the contrary, I detest you—You're a naughty, gawky, foolish Cinderella. You never write me; you don't love your husband; you know what pleasure your letters give him, and yet you haven't written him six lines, dashed off casually!

What do you do all day, Madam? What is the affair so important as to leave you no time to write to your devoted lover? What affection stifles and puts to one side the love, the tender and constant love you promised him? Of what sort can be that marvelous being, that new lover who absorbs every moment, tyrannizes over your days, and prevents your giving any attention to your husband? Josephine, take care! Some fine night, the doors will be broken open, and there I'll be.

Indeed, I am very uneasy, my love, at receiving no news of you; write me quickly four pages, pages full of agreeable things which shall fill my heart with the pleasantest feelings.

I hope before long to crush you in my arms and cover you with a million kisses burning as though beneath the equator.

Bonaparte

THE OWL AND THE PUSSY-CAT

The Owl and the Pussy-Cat went to sea
    In a beautiful pea-green boat;
They took some honey, and plenty of money
    Wrapped up in a five-pound note.
The Owl looked up to the stars above,
    And sang to a small guitar,
"O lovely Pussy, O Pussy, my love,
    What a beautiful Pussy you are,
        You are,
        You are!
    What a beautiful Pussy you are!"

Pussy said to the Owl, "You elegant fowl,
    How charmingly sweet you sing!
Oh! let us be married; too long we have tarried;
    But what shall we do for a ring?"

They sailed away, for a year and a day,
    To the land where the bong-tree grows;
And there in a wood a Piggy-wig stood,
    With a ring at the end of his nose,
        His nose,
        His nose,
    With a ring at the end of his nose.

"Dear Pig, are you willing to sell for one shilling
    Your ring?" Said the Piggy, "I will."
So they took it away, and were married next day
    By the Turkey who lives on the hill.
They dined on mince and slices of quince,
    Which they ate with a runcible spoon;
And hand in hand, on the edge of the sand,
    They danced by the light of the moon,
        The moon,
        The moon,
    They danced by the light of the moon.

EDWARD LEAR

11

SONNET

I wish I could remember that first day,
    First hour, first moment of your meeting me,
    If bright or dim the season, it might be
Summer or winter for aught I can say;
So unrecorded did it slip away,
    So blind was I to see and to foresee,
    So dull to mark the budding of my tree
That would not blossom yet for many a May.
If only I could recollect it, such
    A day of days! I let it come and go
    As traceless as a thaw of bygone snow;
It seemed to mean so little, meant so much;
If only now I could recall that touch,
    First touch of hand in hand—Did one but
    know!

CHRISTINA ROSSETTI

Keats to Fanny Brawne

I never knew before, what such love as you have made me feel, was; I did not believe in it; my Fanny was afraid of it, lest it should burn me up. But if you will fully love me, though there may be some fire 'twill not be more than we can bear when moistened and bedewed with Pleasures.... I love you the more in that I believe you have liked me for my own sake and for nothing else. I have met with women who I really think would like to be married to a Poem and to be given away by a Novel.

Ever yours, my love!

WHEN A
BELOVÈD HAND

When a belovèd hand is laid in ours,
When, jaded with the rush and glare
Of the interminable hours,
Our eyes can in another's eyes read clear,
When our world-deafened ear
Is by the tones of a loved voice caressed,—
A bolt is shot back somewhere in our breast,
And a lost pulse of feeling stirs again.
The eye sinks inward, and the heart lies plain,
And what we mean, we say, and what we would,
     we know!
A man becomes aware of his life's flow,
And hears its winding murmur, and he sees
The meadows where it glides, the sun, the breeze
And there arrives a lull in the hot race,
Wherein he doth for ever chase

That flying and elusive shadow, rest.
An air of coolness plays upon his face,
And an unwonted calm pervades his breast.
And then he thinks he knows
The hills where his life rose,
And the sea where it goes.

MATTHEW ARNOLD

A RED, RED ROSE

My Luve's like a red, red rose
That's newly sprung in June:
O my Luve's like the melodie
That's sweetly play'd in tune!

As fair art thou, my bonnie lass,
So deep in luve am I:
And I will luve thee still, my dear,
Till a' the seas gang dry:

Till a' the seas gang dry, my dear,
And the rocks melt wi' the sun;
I will luve thee still, my dear,
While the sands o'life shall run.

And fare thee weel, my only Luve,
And fare thee weel a while!
And I will come again, my Luve,
Tho' it were ten thousand mile.

ROBERT BURNS

17

THE PASSIONATE SHEPHERD TO HIS LOVE

Come live with me and be
    my Love,
And we will all the pleasures
    prove
That hills and valleys, dales and
    fields,
Or woods or steepy mountain
    yields.

And we will sit upon the rocks,
And see the shepherds feed
    their flocks
By shallow rivers, to whose falls
Melodious birds sing madrigals.

And I will make thee beds of roses
And a thousand fragrant posies;
A cap of flowers, and a kirtle
Embroidered all with leaves of myrtle;

A gown made of the finest wool
Which from our pretty lambs we pull;
Fair-linèd slippers for the cold,
With buckles of the purest gold;

A belt of straw and ivy buds
With coral clasps and amber studs—
And if these pleasures may thee move,
Come live with me and by my Love.

The shepherd swains shall dance and sing
For thy delight each May morning—
If these delights thy mind may move,
Then live with me and be my Love.

CHRISTOPHER MARLOWE

JUNE

Last June I saw your face three times,
    Three times I touched your hand;
Now, as before, May month is o'er,
    And June is in the land.

O many Junes shall come and go,
    Flower-footed o'er the mead;
O many Junes for me, to whom
    Is length of days decreed.

There shall be sunlight, scent of rose.
    Warm mist of Summer rain;
Only this change—I shall not look
    Upon your face again.

AMY LEVY

A Stolen Kiss

Now gentle sleep hath closèd up those eyes
Which, waking, kept my boldest thoughts in awe;
And free access unto that sweet lip lies,
From whence I long the rosy breath to draw.

Methinks no wrong it were, if I should steal
From those two melting rubies one poor kiss;
None sees the theft that would the theft reveal,
Nor rob I her of aught that she can miss;

Nay, should I twenty kisses take away,
There would be little sign I would do so;
Why then should I this robbery delay?
O, she may wake, and therewith angry grow!

Well, if she do, I'll back restore that one,
And twenty hundred thousand more for loan.

GEORGE WITHER

October 15, 1839

My mind is quite made up—and I told
Albert this morning of it; the warm affection
he showed me on learning this gave me _great_
pleasure. He seems _perfection_, and I think
that I have the prospect of very great
happiness before me. I _love_ him _more_ than I
can say... We also think it better, and

Albert quite approves of it, that we should be married very soon after Parliament meets, about the beginning of February; and indeed, loving Albert as I do, I cannot wish it should be delayed. My feelings are a little changed, I must say, since last Spring, when I said I couldn't <u>think</u> of marrying for <u>three or four years</u>; but seeing Albert has changed all this.

ONE-AND-TWENTY

When I was one-and-twenty
I heard a wise man say,
"Give crowns and pounds and guineas
But not your heart away;
Give pearls away and rubies
But keep your fancy free."

But I was one-and-twenty,
  No use to talk to me.
When I was one-and-twenty
  I heard him say again,
"The heart out of the bosom
  Was never given in vain;
'Tis paid with sighs a-plenty
  And sold for endless rue."
And I am two-and-twenty,
  And oh, 'tis true, 'tis true!

A. E. HOUSMAN

Let Me Not to the Marriage of True Minds

Let me not to the marriage of true minds
Admit impediments. Love is not love
Which alters when it alteration finds,
Or bends with the remover to remove:
O, no! it is an ever-fixèd mark
That looks on tempests and is never shaken;
It is the star to every wand'ring bark,
Whose worth's unknown, although his height be taken.
Love's not Time's fool, though rosy lips and cheeks
Within his bending sickle's compass come;
Love alters not with his brief hours and weeks,
But bears it out even to the edge of doom,
If this be error and upon me proved,
I never writ, nor no man ever loved.

WILLIAM SHAKESPEARE

October 19, 1805

My Dearest Beloved
Emma, the dear friend of my
bosom. The signal has been made that the
enemy's combined fleet are coming out of the port. We
have very little wind, so that I have no hopes of seeing
them before tomorrow. May the God of battles crown
my endeavors with success; at all events, I will take
care that my name shall ever be most dear to you and
Horatio, both of whom I love as much as my own life.
And as my last writing, before the battle, will be to
you, so I hope, in God, that I shall live to finish my
letter after the battle. May heaven bless you, prays

your

Nelson

ANNABEL LEE

It was many and many a year ago,
In a kingdom by the sea
That a maiden there lived whom you may know
By the name of Annabel Lee;—
And this maiden she lived with no other thought
Than to love and be loved by me.

I was a child and *she* was a child,
In this kingdom by the sea,
But we loved with a love that was more than love—
I and my Annabel Lee—
With a love that the wingèd seraphs of Heaven
Coveted her and me.

And this was the reason that, long ago,
In this kingdom by the sea,
A wind blew out of a cloud, chilling
My beautiful Annabel Lee;

So that her high-born kinsmen came
And bore her away from me,
To shut her up in a sepulcher
In this kingdom by the sea.

The angels, not half so happy in Heaven,
Went envying her and me,—
Yes!—that was the reason (as all men know,
In this kingdom by the sea)
That the wind came out of the cloud by night,
Chilling and killing my Annabel Lee.

But our love it was stronger by far than the love
Of those who were older than we—
Of many far wiser than we—
And neither the angels in Heaven above,
Nor the demons down under the sea,
Can ever dissever my soul from the soul
Of the beautiful Annabel Lee:—

For the moon never beams without bringing me
    dreams
Of the beautiful Annabel Lee;
And the stars never rise but I feel the bright eyes
Of the beautiful Annabel Lee;
And so, all the night-tide, I lie down by the side
Of my darling,—my darling,—my life and my bride,
In the sepulcher there by the sea—
In her tomb by the sounding sea.

EDGAR ALLAN POE

I think true love is never blind,
    But rather brings an added light,
An inner vision quick to find
    The beauties hid from common sight.

No soul can ever clearly see
    Another's highest, noblest part,
Save through the sweet philosophy
    And loving wisdom of the heart.

PHOEBE CARY

My Dearest
Teresa,——I have read this
book in your garden;——my love, you were
absent, or else I could not have read it. It is a
favorite book of yours, and the writer was a friend of
mine. You will not understand these English words,
and _others_ will not understand them,——which is the
reason I have not scrawled them in Italian. But you
will recognize the handwriting of him who
passionately loved you, and you will divine that, over a
book which was yours, he could only think of love.

In that word, beautiful in all languages, but most so in

32

yours—*Amor mio*—is comprised my existence here and hereafter. I feel I exist here, and I feel that I shall exist hereafter,—to *what* purpose you will decide; my destiny rests with you, and you are a woman, eighteen years of age, and two out of a convent. I wish that you had staid there, with all my heart,—or, at least, that I had never met you in your married state.

But all this is too late. I love you, and you love me,—at least, you *say* so, and *act* as if you *did* so, which last is a great consolation in all events. But *I* more than love you, and cannot cease to love you.

Think of me, sometimes, when the Alps and ocean divide us,—but they never will, unless you *wish* it.

WE'LL GO
NO MORE

So, we'll go no more a-roving
So late into the night,
Though the heart be still as loving,
And the moon be still as bright.

For the sword outwears its sheath,
And the soul wears out the breast,
And the heart must pause to breathe,
And love itself have rest.

Though the night was made for loving,
And the day returns too soon,
Yet we'll go no more a-roving
By the light of the moon.

LORD BYRON

35

July 17, 1796

I have received your
letter, my adorable; it has
filled my heart with joy. I am
grateful for the trouble you have taken to
give me your news. Your health should be better
today; I feel sure you have recovered. I urge you
to go riding; that can't fail to do you good.

...I will send your horse; but I hope you will
soon be able to join me. A few days ago I thought
I loved you; but since I last saw you I feel I love
you a thousand times more. All the time I have

known you I adore you more each day; that just shows how wrong was La Bruyère's maxim that <u>love comes all at once</u>. Everything in Nature has its own life and different stages of growth. I beg you, let me see some of your faults: be less beautiful, less graceful, less kind, less good; but, above all, never be jealous and never cry; your tears drive me mad and burn my blood. Be sure I can't have a thought except of you or an idea I don't tell you about.

Rest thoroughly and get well. Come and join me; before we die let us at least be able to say: "We had so many happy days!!"

GIVE ALL
TO LOVE

Give all to love;
Obey thy heart;
Friends, kindred, days,
Estate, good-fame,
Plans, credit, and the Muse,—
Nothing refuse.

'Tis a brave master;
Let it have scope:
Follow it utterly,
Hope beyond hope:
High and more high
It dives into noon,
With wing unspent,
Untold intent;
But it is a god,
Knows its own path,
And the outlets of the sky.

It was not for the mean;
It requireth courage stout,
Souls above doubt,
Valor unbending;
It will reward,—
They shall return
More than they were,
And ever ascending.

Leave all for love;
Yet, hear me, yet,
One word more thy heart behoved,
One pulse more of firm endeavor,—
Keep thee today,
To-morrow, forever,
Free as an Arab
Of thy beloved.

Cling with life to the maid;
But when the surprise,
First vague shadow of surmise
Flits across her bosom young
Of a joy apart from thee,
Free be she, fancy-free;
Nor thou detain her vesture's hem,
Nor the palest rose she flung
From her summer diadem.

RALPH WALDO EMERSON

LOVE

I love you,
Not only for what you are,
But for what I am
When I am with you.

I love you,
Not only for what
You have made of yourself,
But for what
You are making of me.

I love you
For the part of me
That you bring out;
I love you
For putting your hand
Into my heaped-up heart
And passing over

All the foolish, weak things
That you can't help
Dimly seeing there,
And for drawing out
Into the light
All the beautiful belongings
That no one else had looked
Quite far enough to find.

I love you because you
Are helping me to make
Of the lumber of my life
Not a tavern
But a temple;
Out of the works
Of my every day
Not a reproach
But a song.

I love you
Because you have done
More than any creed
Could have done
To make me good,
And more than any fate
Could have done
To make me happy.

You have done it
Without a touch,
Without a word,
Without a sign.
You have done it
By being yourself.
Perhaps that is what
Being a friend means,
After all.

ROY CROFT

43

Good Morning

Though still in bed my thoughts go out to
you, my Immortal Beloved, now and then
joyfully, then sadly, waiting to learn whether

or not fate will hear us. I can live only
wholly with you or not at all—yes, I am
resolved to wander so long away from you
until I can fly to your arms and say that I
am really at home, send my soul enwrapped
in you into the land of spirits.—Yes,
unhappily it must be so—you will be the
more resolved since you know my fidelity—
to you, no one can ever again possess my
heart—none—never—Oh, God! why is it
necessary to part from one whom one so loves

and yet my life in W. [Vienna] is now a wretched life—your love makes me at once the happiest and the unhappiest of men—at my age, I need a steady, quiet life—can that be under our conditions? My angel, I have just been told that the mail coach goes every day—and I must close at once so that you may receive the L. at once. Be calm, only by a calm consideration of our existence can we achieve our purpose to live together.—be calm—love me—today—

46

yesterday—what tearful longings for you—
you—you—my life—my all—farewell—
Oh continue to love me—never misjudge the
most faithful heart of
your beloved L.
ever thine
ever mine
ever for each other.

$\mathcal{Y}$ou bound strong sandals on my feet,
You gave me bread and wine,
And sent me under sun and stars,
For all the world was mine.

Oh take the sandals off my feet,
You know not what to do;
For all my world is in your arms,
My sun and stars are you.

SARA TEASDALE

48

To My Dear and Loving Husband

If ever two were one, then surely we.
If ever man were lov'd by wife, then thee.
If ever wife was happy in a man,
Compare with me, ye women, if you can.
I prize thy love more than whole Mines of gold,
Or all the riches that the East doth hold.
My love is such that Rivers cannot quench,
Nor ought but love from thee give recompence.
Thy love is such I can no way repay;
The heavens reward thee manifold I pray.
Then while we live, in love lets so persever,
That when we live no more, we may live ever.

ANNE BRADSTREET

GATHER YE ROSEBUDS

Gather ye rosebuds while ye may,
Old Time is still a-flying;
And this same flower that smiles today
Tomorrow will be dying.

The glorious lamp of heaven, the Sun,
The higher he's a-getting,
The sooner will his race be run,
And nearer he's to setting.

That age is best, which is the first,
When youth and blood are warmer
But being spent, the worst, and worst
Times still succeed the former.

Then be not coy, but use your time,
And while you may, go marry:
For having lost but once your prime
You may for ever tarry.

ROBERT HERRICK

1915

My Precious Darling,

My warm and loving thanks for your dear letter, full
of tender words, and for both telegrams. I too have
you in my thoughts on this our 21st anniversary! I
wish you health and all that a deeply loving heart can
desire, and thank you on my knees for all your love,

affection, friendship and patience, which you have shown me during these long years of our married life!

Today's weather reminds me of that day in Coburg— how sad it is that we are not together! Nobody knew that it was the day of our betrothal—it is strange how soon people forget—besides, it means nothing to them...

Before the evening I drove along the old road to the town of Slonin in the province of Grodno. It was extraordinarily warm and pleasant; and the smell of the pine forest—one feels enervated and softened!

Always your hubby,

Nicky

BELIEVE ME
IF ALL THOSE
ENDEARING
YOUNG CHARMS

*B*elieve me, if all those endearing young charms
Which I gaze on so fondly today
Were to fade by tomorrow and fleet in my arms
Like fairy gifts fading away,
Thou wouldst still be adored as this moment
      thou art,
Let thy loveliness fade as it will,
And around the dear ruin each wish of my heart
Would entwine itself verdantly still.

It is not while beauty and youth are thine own
And thy cheeks unprofaned by a tear
That the fervor and faith of a soul can be known
To which time will but make thee more dear.

No, the heart that has truly loved never forgets
But as truly loves on to the close—
As the sunflower turns on her god when he sets
The same look which she turned when he rose.

THOMAS MOORE

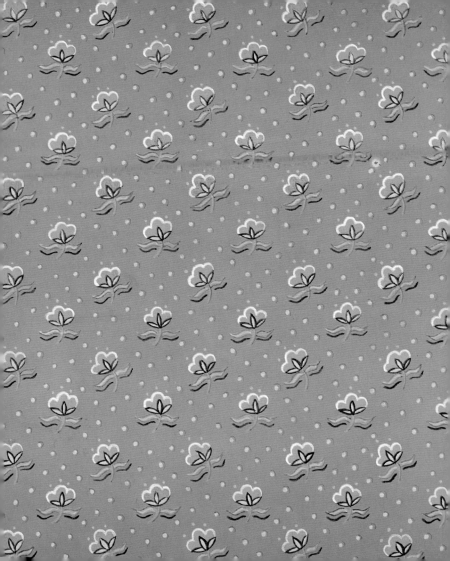